GOOD
SAINT JOSEPH

By REV. LAWRENCE G. LOVASIK, S.V.D.
Divine Word Missionary

CATHOLIC BOOK PUBLISHING CORP.
TOTOWA, NJ

AN ANGEL APPEARS
TO JOSEPH

JOSEPH was a young carpenter in the town of Nazareth. All knew him to be a very good man who loved God and served Him faithfully. He was about to marry Mary, a young girl in the same town.

The Angel Gabriel appeared to Mary and told her that God wanted her to become the Mother of His Son. She said, "I am the servant of the Lord. Let it be done to me as you say." At that moment she became the Mother of God. The Second Person of the Blessed Trinity took to Himself a body and soul like ours. He became Man and lived among us.

Joseph did not know about the visit of the Angel Gabriel, so he wanted to leave Mary when he learned that she was to have a Child.

Nihil Obstat: Daniel V. Flynn, J.C.D., *Censor Librorum*
Imprimatur: ✠ James P. Mahoney, *Vicar General, Archdiocese of New York*
© 1978 *Catholic Book Publishing Corp., Totowa, N.J.*
Printed in China   ISBN 978-0-89942-283-1
CPSIA   December 2020   10 9 8 7 6 5 4   L/P

An Angel appeared to Joseph in a dream, saying, "Joseph, son of David, have no fear about taking Mary as your wife. It is by the Holy Spirit that she has conceived this Child. She is to have a Son and you are to name Him Jesus because He will save His people from their sins."

When Joseph awoke, he did as the Angel of the Lord told him and received Mary into his home as his wife.

MARY AND JOSEPH ARE MARRIED

MARY and Joseph appeared before the priest in the Temple. Joseph became the true husband of the Virgin Mary. They made their home in Nazareth.

Mary and Joseph were deeply devoted to each other. No one after God loved Joseph as much as Mary did. She saw in him a just man, close to God—kind, pure and devoted.

After God, no one loved Mary as much as Joseph did. He admired her wonderful beauty of body and soul, and looked forward to the honor of spending his life making his loving wife happy.

Mary and Joseph are an example of the kind of love husbands and wives should have for each other.

MARY AND JOSEPH GO TO BETHLEHEM

THE Roman Emperor Augustus ordered all the people to be counted in the places from which their families had come. Mary and Joseph, being of the family of David, left their home in Nazareth and traveled to Bethlehem.

The town of Bethlehem was crowded. There was no room in the inn, where travelers could spend the night. Joseph was told that he could take his wife to a stable, where the animals of the travelers were kept.

Joseph was very sad that he could not find a better place for his wife, where she could peacefully rest for the night. The great love that Mary and Joseph had for each other was enough to make this stable a home. They were to share many more hardships together because God had chosen them to have a part in the work of our salvation in close union with Jesus, the Messiah, Whose coming the people of God were awaiting.

JOSEPH ADORES THE INFANT JESUS

WHILE Mary and Joseph were in the stable of Bethlehem, Mary gave birth to her Son, wrapped Him in soft clothes and laid Him in a manger, where the cows, donkeys and oxen were fed.

Joseph knew that this Child was the Son of God and the Savior of the world, of Whom the prophets of the Old Testament had spoken so many times. He was happy to see Jesus, Who was truly Mary's Son. Both adored the Divine Infant.

THE COMING OF THE SHEPHERDS

SHEPHERDS were tending their sheep in a field near Bethlehem.

Suddenly an Angel appeared and said, "You have nothing to fear! I come to bring you good news of great joy to be shared by the whole people. This day in David's city a Savior has been born to you, the Messiah and Lord. Let this be a sign to you: In a manger you will find an Infant wrapped in swaddling clothes."

Then, there were with the Angel many more Angels, praising God and saying, "Glory to God in high heaven, peace on earth to those on whom His favor rests."

When the Angels had returned to heaven, the shepherds said to one another, "Let us go over to Bethlehem and see this event, which the Lord has made known to us." They went in haste and found Mary and Joseph, and the Baby lying in the manger. Once the shepherds saw, they understood what the Angels told them about this Child.

JOSEPH GIVES JESUS HIS NAME

EIGHT days after the birth of the Child, the name "Jesus" was given to Him because the Angel told Joseph in a dream, "You are to name Him Jesus because He will save His people from their sins."

The name "Jesus" means "Savior." This was the first time that Jesus shed His Blood for us.

JOSEPH TAKES MARY AND HER CHILD TO THE TEMPLE

IT WAS the law among the Jews that the first child born in a family should be brought to the Temple to be offered to God because he belonged to God. When Jesus was forty days old, Mary and Joseph brought Him to the Temple.

There lived in Jerusalem a pious man named Simeon, and the Holy Spirit, Who revealed to him that he would not die until he had seen the Messiah, was upon him. Simeon went to the Temple, inspired by the Holy Spirit. When the parents brought in the Child Jesus to offer Him to God, he took Jesus in his arms and thanked God in these words, "Now Master, You can take Your servant to Yourself in peace. You have kept Your promise. My eyes have seen the Promised Savior, the Light to all nations and the Glory of Your people Israel."

Then Simeon said to Mary, "This Child will bring salvation to many, and you will be pierced with a sword of suffering."

Joseph wondered what the old Simeon meant. He was ready to stand by Jesus and Mary in any suffering that God may have wanted them to bear to save all.

JOSEPH WELCOMES THE MAGI

AFTER the birth of Jesus, during the rule of King Herod, some very learned men, called Magi, arrived in Jerusalem from the east, asking, "Where is the newborn King of the Jews? We saw His star and have come to honor Him."

King Herod was afraid, and so were many people in Jerusalem, when they heard that a new King was born. Herod found out from the priests that the Messiah was to be born in Bethlehem. Herod asked the Magi to let him know if they found the new King.

The Magi saw the star again, which led them to the house where they found the Child with Mary, His Mother, and Joseph. They bowed before Him and then gave Him gifts of gold and rich spices.

In a dream they were told not to return to Herod, so they went back to their own country by another way. All this made Joseph very happy, for he believed that someday even the people who had faith in God would know and love Jesus.

JOSEPH TAKES JESUS AND
MARY INTO EGYPT

SOON after the Magi had gone away, God sent
an Angel to Joseph, who said to him in a
dream, "Get up and take the Child and His
Mother, and flee to Egypt. Stay there until I tell
you. Herod wants to kill the Child."

King Herod sent out his soldiers to Bethlehem and ordered them to kill all the little children there who were two years old or younger. He wanted to be sure that he would kill Jesus. But Jesus was safe in the loving care of good Saint Joseph.

JOSEPH RETURNS TO NAZARETH

AFTER Herod's death, the Angel of the Lord appeared in a dream to Joseph in Egypt with the command, "Get up, take the Child and His Mother and set out for the land of Israel. Those who wanted to take the life of the Child are dead."

Joseph got up, took the Child and His Mother, and returned to the land of Israel. He made his home in a town called Nazareth.

Joseph's happiest moments were spent with Jesus and Mary. Mary often visited him in the carpenter shop. He felt honored to work hard for the Son of God and His loving Mother. No one ever loved Jesus and Mary as Joseph did. They were his whole life.

Mary and Joseph often thought of Jesus and loved Him more each day. In their hearts they wondered at His holiness and silently adored Him. All the while Jesus was making their souls holier and more beautiful, because He was giving them His grace.

JOSEPH FINDS THE BOY JESUS
IN THE TEMPLE

MARY and Joseph used to go every year to Jerusalem for the feast of the Passover. When Jesus was twelve they went up for the celebration. As they were returning at the end of the feast, the Child Jesus remained behind and His parents did not know it. Thinking He was in another group of travelers, they continued their journey for a day. Then they looked for Jesus among His relatives and friends.

Since Mary and Joseph could not find Him, they returned to Jerusalem to look for Him. On the third day, they found Him in the Temple sitting with the teachers, listening to them and asking them questions. All who heard Him were surprised to see how much He knew about God.

When His parents saw Him they were surprised, and His Mother said to Him, "Son, why have You done this to us? You see that Your father and I have been searching for You in sorrow."

He said to them, "Why did you search for Me? Did you not know I had to be in My Father's house?"

Jesus went down with Mary and Joseph and came to Nazareth. He was obedient to them. In this He is an example for all boys and girls who must love and obey their parents because this is the Fourth Commandment of God. **21**

JESUS WORKS WITH JOSEPH

AS JESUS became older, He also grew in wisdom and age and grace before God and men.

Jesus helped His Mother in the home and learned the trade of a carpenter from His foster father, Saint Joseph. In the same way boys and girls must help their parents.

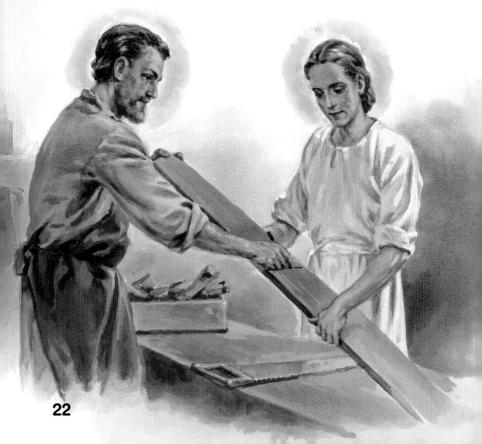

Jesus worked beside His foster father, Saint Joseph, whom He obeyed as His own Father in heaven. He knew that Joseph was taking His heavenly Father's place on earth. And Joseph knew that the Boy in his care was the all-powerful Son of God and that Mary, his wife, was the Mother of God. He loved them with all his heart. He worked long hours in his carpenter shop to give Jesus and Mary what they needed. God chose a carpenter to be the foster father of Jesus to show us how much He honored work. Saint Joseph is the patron of workers.

Your whole life should be devoted to Jesus and Mary as Joseph's was. Ask him to help you to love Jesus and Mary as he did. You love Jesus and Mary not only by praying to them often, but also by trying to please them in all that you do as Joseph did. Pray for your father, who works so hard to take care of your family, that Saint Joseph may help him in his work.

JOSEPH WAS THE HEAD
OF THE HOLY FAMILY

GOD chose Joseph to be the foster father of His Son, the husband of Mary, and the head of the Holy Family because he was a holy man. God gave him all the graces he needed to be a worthy head of the holiest family on earth.

Joseph admired the beautiful example that Jesus and Mary gave him. Like them, he obeyed the will of God in all things. He served Jesus and Mary for the love of God.

The Holy Family found their happiness in loving and serving God faithfully. They often prayed together and read the writings of the Old Testament. They found their peace and joy in God alone.

The Holy Family is an example of a prayerful family that all Catholic families should imitate. Pray to Jesus, Mary and Joseph for your own family that you may find peace and joy in God alone and serve Him with all the love of your heart as the Holy Family of Nazareth did.

THE DEATH OF JOSEPH

IN THE quiet village of Nazareth, Joseph lived his life, working in the carpenter shop and going to the synagogue to pray. It was a life of humble obedience, prayer and work.

One day, God called his servant Joseph to heaven. He died a happy death in the arms of Jesus and Mary, whom he had loved and served so faithfully.

After Joseph's death, Jesus, Who was still a young man, took care of His Mother Mary. Jesus worked as a carpenter as His foster father had done.

The Church has chosen Saint Joseph to be the special patron of a happy death. Pray to Joseph—for yourself and your whole family—so that when the hour of death comes, you too may die in the arms of Jesus and Mary.

<u>Say this prayer each day:</u>

Jesus, Mary, and Joseph, I give you my heart and my soul.

Jesus, Mary, and Joseph, help me in my last agony.

Jesus, Mary, and Joseph, may I die in peace with you.

SAINT JOSEPH IS THE
PROTECTOR OF FAMILIES

GOD placed His own Son and His Mother under the loving care of Saint Joseph. Since he was so faithful in the work God gave him to do, He wanted Joseph to be the protector of all Christian families. And Saint Joseph wants nothing more than to lead families to God by his example and by his prayers in heaven.

Pray to Saint Joseph for your whole family because he loves all of you for the sake of Jesus and Mary. Ask him to protect your family from all sin—which makes a family unhappy. Ask him to help all of you to love Jesus and Mary as he did so that your family may be like the Holy Family of Nazareth and be together in heaven someday.

SAINT JOSEPH IS THE PROTECTOR OF THE CHURCH

THE Catholic Church is the family of God, for we are all God's children, especially through Holy Baptism. As God made Joseph the protector of his Holy Family at Nazareth, so God wishes him to be the protector of His Church on earth.

Saint Joseph's power in heaven is very great because he is the foster father of the Savior of the world, and the husband of Mary, the Mother of God and Queen of heaven and earth. He was the obedient servant of the heavenly Father and took His place upon earth.

Pray to Saint Joseph for the Holy Father and for the Bishops and priests of the Catholic Church. Pray for all Catholics, that they may live a holy life and that they may be a good example to all.

Pray to Saint Joseph that the Catholic Church may spread everywhere in the world, so that all may learn about the true Faith that Jesus has given us through His Church.

PRAYER TO SAINT JOSEPH

GOOD Saint Joseph, I want you to be my special friend.

I honor you as the servant of God the Father, the foster father of Jesus Christ, and the loving husband of the Blessed Virgin Mary. I honor you as the patron of families and the protector of the Catholic Church.

Into your care I place my soul and my body. Keep me from all sin, and help me to love God with all my heart, and my neighbor for the love of God, just as you always did.

Give me a great love for Jesus and Mary, above all by praying to them often.

Help those whom I love, my parents, and my brothers and sisters, and those who are good to me. Pray for us that we may serve God faithfully on earth and may see God forever in heaven. Through your prayers may our whole family be happy with your Holy Family in heaven forever. Amen.